"Can I Just Stop You There.."

The M7 Steps To Confident Success

By

MARIE MITCHELL
Sales and Self-Confidence
Strategies for Success

Copyright © 2024 Marie Mitchell

All rights reserved.

ISBN: 9798325837098

Imprint: Independently published

DEDICATION

Dylan,

My Grandson, your endless zest for self-improvement breathed life into these pages. You challenged me to keep moving, to keep believing, even when I stumbled. This book is a tribute to your spirit, a celebration of your unwavering determination. May it inspire you to keep chasing your dreams, my fearless adventurer.

With all my love,
Mitch x

CONTENTS

Chapter		Page
1	Introduction	7
2	Step 1 Planning and Prep	11
3	Step 2 Customer Contact	13
4	Step 3 Fact Finding	16
5	Step 4 Solution	20
6	Step 5 Objections	24
7	Step 6 Close	30
8	M7: Follow Up - Building Lasting Relationships	32
Summary	Summery of the steps	34
Author	About the author	36

CHAPTER 1

Introduction

Have you ever felt the icy grip of fear as a prospect's hand drifts toward the "mute" button mid-sentence?

That sinking feeling when their glazed eyes scream, "Please, just stop talking"?

When you're mid-sentence in your telephone pitch and you hear those fateful words,

"Can I just stop you there?..."

Yeah, we've all been there. It's the sales equivalent of walking into a room wearing mismatched socks – embarrassing, confidence-crushing, and a surefire way to kill the deal.

But here's the good news: those days are over.

This isn't your old boss's dusty sales manual.
No, this is the M7 Sales Track: your roadmap to obliterating awkward silences, turning objections into opportunities, and leaving prospects begging for more (yes, you read that right, begging).

This isn't just about closing deals, though. It's about transforming you into a sales force to be reckoned with.

You'll become a Master of Communication, a magician of persuasion, and a champion of customer needs.

So, whether you're a seasoned veteran or a fresh-faced rookie, buckle up, because the M7 Sales Track is about to launch you into an endless stream of sales successes. I'm not just promising to turn you into a salesperson, I'm guaranteeing it.

Are you ready to ditch the sock mismatches and step into the spotlight? Then open this book, embrace the M7 way, and get ready to hear those sweet, sweet words: "Sold!"

I always say that getting that perfect sale is a bit like baking a cake.
If I were to bake (and I can't) I'd get my butter, my sugar, my flour - throw them into a bowl, give it a quick stir and throw into the oven. And I would expect it to come out as a Victoria Sponge to rival anything I could buy at M&S. But of course, it wouldn't.

Selling is exactly the same.

Sure, you might have a vague idea of the ingredients and the steps involved. You might even have a picture of the finished product in your mind. But without a clear roadmap, your cake is likely to turn out a gooey mess, or worse, a burnt disaster.

Selling is no different from baking a cake. It's a process that requires precision, timing, and the right ingredients. And just like a cake, if you don't follow the recipe, you're not going to get the results you want.

That's where the M7 comes in.

It's the 7 essential steps you need to take, in the right order, to bake the perfect sales cake. It's your roadmap to success, your guide to turning prospects into customers, and your key to unlocking the top of the sales mountain.

Think of the M7 as your secret sales weapon. It's the difference between a fumbled pitch and a closed deal. It's the knowledge that separates the amateurs from the masters.

In this book, you'll discover:

- The 7 key ingredients of every successful sale.

- The exact steps you need to take to move your prospect through the sales funnel.

- Proven strategies for building rapport, overcoming objections, and closing the deal.

- Actionable tips to avoid common sales pitfalls.

- Real-world examples of the M7 in action.

By the end of this book, you'll be able to:

- Craft compelling sales presentations.

- Build trust and rapport with your prospects.

- Handle objections with confidence.

- Close deals like a pro.

So why is it called M7?

For so many years as a Sales Trainer I've watched countless faces light up as they reached the summit of a closed sale. But the climb wasn't always graceful. It took countless stumbles, detours, and lessons learned to forge the path I now call the M7.

More than just a catchy acronym, "M" stands for Maz, my journey etched into each step. This book is the blueprint, the map I wish I had when I first tackled the treacherous terrain of sales.

It's not about shortcuts or empty pitches; it's about genuine connection, uncovering needs, and crafting solutions that bloom into mutual success. Forget fleeting victories – the M7 is a rope ladder to lasting customer loyalty.

Ready to reach the summit of the M7?

Take the first step with me. Let's climb together.

CHAPTER 2

Step 1 Planning and Prep

Ah, yes, the foundation of any sales magic: Planning and Preparation! Before we delve into the firestorm of the M7, we must first gather our ingredients and meticulously set the stage. Remember when I said it was like baking a cake, we have all the right ingredients- well our planning is a bit like ensuring the perfect heat and environment for this amazing transformation to occur.

Here's how planning and preparation set you up for M7 mastery:

1. Know Your Product Inside Out:
You wouldn't expect an alchemist to work with unknown elements, would you? Similarly, thorough product knowledge is your bedrock. Understand its features, benefits, and nuances like the back of your hand. Be ready to answer any question, anticipate objections, and confidently showcase its value proposition.

2. Research Your Customer:
Every person is unique, and so are their needs. Dive deep into your target audience. Understand their demographics, challenges, aspirations, and buying habits. The more you know, the more effectively you can personalise your M7 approach.

3. Set Measurable Goals:
Vague dreams rarely turn into gold. Define your sales goals clearly and quantify them. This could be specific numbers of sales, revenue targets, or conversion rates. Having actionable goals keeps you focused and allows you to track your progress through the M7 journey.

4. Craft Your Pitch:
Words are your tools, and your pitch is your masterpiece. Craft a compelling message that resonates with your target audience. Highlight the benefits, paint a vivid picture of their lives with your product, and practice delivering it with confidence and enthusiasm.

5. Anticipate Objections:
Objections are like impurities in the gold. They're inevitable, but manageable. Prepare common responses to price concerns, feature comparisons, and logistical hurdles. By addressing them head-on, you can turn these obstacles into opportunities to showcase your expertise and build trust.

6. Prepare Your Tools:
You have your CRM, sales collateral, and presentation materials. Ensure everything is organised, accessible, and visually appealing.

Remember, professionalism matters, and first impressions leave lasting impressions.

Planning and preparation aren't glamorous, but they're the invisible magic behind the M7's brilliance. With a solid foundation, you enter the crucible of sales ready to transform, ready to turn hesitant prospects into loyal customers, and ultimately, to forge your own success story.

Now, with the everything prepped and the tools at hand, let's dive into the heart of the M7 process!

Eager to get started?

Then let's go find out what Step 2 is!

CHAPTER 3

Step 2 Customer Contact

Imagine this: you're standing at the edge of a vast, uncharted ocean. The waves lap at your feet, a salty breeze whispers secrets in your ear, and before you stretch a limitless horizon of possibilities.

That, my friend, is the world of customer contact. It's the bridge between businesses and their lifeblood – their customers. It's the first spark that ignites a relationship, the handshake that seals a deal, the whisper that builds trust.

So, what exactly is this enigmatic "customer contact?"
Simply put, it's the multifaceted interaction between a business and its audience. It's the smile of a barista greeting you in the morning, the helpful email from a tech support agent calming your tech-induced panic, the persuasive voice on the phone offering a solution to your woes.

It encompasses every touchpoint, every channel – phone calls, emails, social media, face-to-face meetings – where a business engages with its potential or existing customers.

But customer contact isn't just about transactions and information exchange. It's about building rapport, forging connections, and fostering trust. It's about understanding needs, addressing concerns, and exceeding expectations. It's the emotional glue that binds a business to its customer base, creating loyal brand advocates and driving sustainable growth.

Think of it this way: every customer contact is a mini performance, a chance to leave a lasting impression. Like a skilled actor, we navigate the stage, adapting our tone, language, and approach to suit the audience. We weave stories, spark curiosity, and offer solutions with the finesse of a magician pulling a rabbit from a hat.

Why is mastering this art so crucial?
In today's hyper-connected world, competition is fierce. Customers have more choices than ever before, and their loyalty is fickle. A single negative interaction can sour their perception, while a positive one can turn them into raving fans. Customer contact is not just a department, it's a philosophy – a commitment to understanding and exceeding customer expectations at every turn.

The first 40 seconds in tele sales are critical for grabbing your prospect's attention and building rapport. Face to face and Zoom, a little easier - but on any approach ditch the Eeyore routine and let's inject some personality and intrigue into your opening.

Here are some tips:

Ditch the generic:
Instead of "How are you today?", try:
"Good morning! Did you manage to escape
the Scottish deluge this morning?" (if it's raining in Scotland)

"Hope you're enjoying the sunshine after
that wild week of weather!" (if it's sunny)

"Catching my breath after a jam-packed morning.
How's your day shaping up?"

Replace "My name is..." with:
"I'm [Your Name] from [Company], reaching out because..."

"I'm calling about [Relevant topic] - something
I know is on the minds of businesses
like yours in [Prospect's location]."

Spark curiosity:
Instead of launching into your pitch, tease them with a hint:
"I'm working on a project that helps businesses in [Industry] [Achieve something desirable] -
would you be interested in hearing more about it?"

"I came across a recent study that
showed [Interesting statistic] about
[Prospect's industry]. Did you see it?"

"I have a quick question about
[Something related to their business]."

Be genuine and enthusiastic:
- Smile! It translates through your voice.
- Speak clearly and with energy.
- Show genuine interest in their response to your opening.

Remember, this is just the first step:
- Keep it light and avoid getting bogged down in details.

Your goal is to pique their interest and open the door for a deeper conversation.

Listen actively and be prepared to adapt your approach based on their response.

By applying these tips, you can transform your introduction from a snooze-fest to a springboard for a successful conversation. And remember, practice makes perfect!

Ready to find out what's next?
Turn the page!

CHAPTER 4

Step 3 Fact Finding

Fact Finding - digging for the truth in Your Sales Pitch

In the thrilling journey of a successful sales pitch, Step 3 on the M7 unveils the art of Fact Finding, the essential skill that transforms prospecting from a one-sided monologue to a collaborative treasure hunt.

It's not about bombarding your prospect with questions; it's about wielding the magic wand of inquiry to unearth the hidden needs and desires fuelling their decisions.

Why Unmask the Truth?

Forget flashy features and slick pitches. In the world of M7 sales, the true path to success starts with one crucial step: unearthing and establishing needs. And trust me, no prospect will ever buy unless they truly believe they need it.

Wants and needs are two very different things, for example I need a new car. I want a Mercedes. My budget is limited.

Needs are essential for your survival, like food and shelter. They're non-negotiables. Wants, though tempting, are extras that make life enjoyable but aren't crucial.

It's like choosing between water and a fancy bottle – both quench thirst, but only one keeps you alive.

But here's the secret -

Understanding the M7 and using clever fact-finding can be a powerful strategy to uncover hidden needs in your prospects and subtly guide them towards realising your product is the perfect solution.

Through strategic questions and active listening, we uncover the anxieties, frustrations, and aspirations that drive purchase decisions. This isn't about interrogation; it's about building trust and understanding the unique landscape of each prospect.

Why is this so critical?

People buy to solve problems, not collect features.
Our security system isn't just a product; it's peace of mind for families fearing break-ins.

Our marketing software isn't just lines of code; it's the key to unlocking untapped growth potential.

By pinpointing these core needs, we can craft personalised pitches that resonate deeply. We become advisors, not salespeople, demonstrating how our product becomes the missing piece – the solution to their specific challenges and the stepping stone to their desired future.

Building sales on this foundation of need, we forge deep trust and lasting relationships. It's not about fleeting fads, but about understanding the eternal human desire to solve problems and achieve dreams.

Master this art of the M7 and you'll build a successful sales career.

The Art of Questioning:

Your arsenal of questions holds the keys to this. Think of them as tools, each serving a specific purpose:

Open-ended questions Like gentle crowbars, they pry open conversations, inviting elaborate answers.

"What are your biggest frustrations with your current situation?"
or
"What would your ideal solution look like?" are your allies in understanding their landscape.

Open ended questions are information gatherers, and always start with Who, What, Where, When, Why, How. They can be backed up with little phrases like Show me, Tell me.

Closed-ended questions:
These precise drills gather specific data, confirming details and gauging potential roadblocks.
"Do you have a budget in mind?" or
"Have you considered similar solutions before?"
help you navigate the terrain.

Closed questions won't give you much information but will usually offer only Yes or No answer. This can be a fabulous little tool when you need affirmation on a point that you want the prospect to focus on.

Probing questions:
Think of them as magnifying glasses, allowing you to delve deeper into the heart of an answer.
"Can you elaborate on that?" or
"Why is that important to you?"
shed light on the hidden motivations driving their decisions.

Remember:
Active listening is your superpower. Pay close attention to both the spoken word and the unspoken language of body language and tone. God gave us Salespeople two ears and one mouth for a reason - we should be listening twice as much as we speak!

Clarification is your friend. Don't hesitate to ask for further explanation or follow-up questions. It shows genuine interest and ensures understanding.

Neutrality is your shield. Avoid leading questions or pushing your agenda. Let the conversation flow organically, and the needs will reveal themselves.

By wielding the art of questioning and embracing active listening, you transform fact finding from a mere formality into a powerful tool. You build trust, unearth hidden needs, and tailor your pitch to resonate like a perfectly tuned violin.

So, by stepping into Step 3 of M7 with an open mind and a curious spirit, you will watch your sales pitch blossom into a symphony of success.

This chapter is an invitation to embark on a thrilling journey of discovery, where you, the skilled salesperson, hold the map to hidden treasures.

Remember, your questions are your tools, and your active listening is your compass.

As you delve into the heart of your prospect's needs, you'll craft a pitch that shines brighter than any diamond, paving the way for a mutually beneficial and long-lasting collaboration.

Ready for the next step?

CHAPTER 5

Step 4 Solution

So, you've done a thorough fact find with your prospect using a good mix of questioning, you've have good rapport and have been able to build trust and relationship. And you've established the need.

So -what comes next?

Absolutely! You're right on track. We provide the solution- your product!

After qualifying the prospect's needs and building trust, the next crucial step is proving the value of your solution.

Here are some effective ways to do that:

1. Tailor your solution to their specific needs:
Don't offer a generic pitch. Revisit the information you gathered during the fact-find and tailor your solution to address their specific pain points, challenges, and desired outcomes. Highlight how your offering directly solves their problems and meets their unique requirements.

2. Use data and evidence:
Back up your claims with concrete data, case studies, testimonials, and success stories. Share how your solution has helped similar businesses or clients achieve measurable results. Quantify the potential benefits, like increased revenue, reduced costs, or improved efficiency.

3. Offer a proof of concept (POC):
For complex solutions, consider proposing a POC. This gives the prospect a hands-on experience with your product or service in their own environment. It allows them to test its functionality, assess its suitability, and see tangible results before committing to a full purchase.

4. Conduct a value demonstration:
If a POC isn't feasible, a value demonstration can be effective. Showcase how your solution works and highlight its features in a way that directly connects to the prospect's needs. Use simulations, prototypes, or interactive tools to give them a clear understanding of its potential impact.

5. Focus on outcomes, not features:
Remember, it's not about the features; it's about the outcomes. Translate your solution's technical specifications into tangible benefits that resonate with the prospect. Show them how your offering will improve their business, streamline processes, and ultimately help them achieve their goals.

6. Personalise your solution presentation:
There are also fantastic ways you can personalise your solution presentation and make it truly resonate with the prospect. By using phrases like "so what this means for you, Jim" or "So what this means for you and your company, Mrs. Jones," you're essentially translating your offering into the prospect's language and showing them how it directly impacts them.

7. Closed-ended questions:
Closed-ended questions are powerful tools for confirming understanding and gauging the prospect's reaction. By strategically placing them after key points and personalised statements, you can:

> **Ensure clarity:** Closed questions require a definitive answer, forcing the prospect to engage and clarify any confusion. "So what this means for you, Jim, is increased efficiency and a 20% boost in output. Does that sound right?"

Build consensus: When asking "Are you seeing how this will benefit you, Mrs. Jones?", you're inviting agreement and building a shared understanding of the solution's value.

Control the pace: Closed questions allow you to control the conversation flow and ensure you cover all the critical points before moving on.

Here are some additional closed-question examples, tailored to different needs:

Cost saving: "By implementing our automated process, we can save you £X per month. Would that be significant enough to justify the investment?"

Time saving: "With our solution, you could cut your turnaround time by Y%. Would that free up valuable resources for your team?"

Risk mitigation: "Our proven track record and security measures ensure minimal risk for your company. Does that give you peace of mind?

Remember, balance is key. Don't bombard the prospect with questions, but strategically use them to confirm understanding, gauge interest, and identify potential roadblocks.

Combine personalized statements like "So what this means for you..." with questions like "Does that sound like a good fit for your needs?" to create a dynamic and interactive dialogue that builds trust and moves the prospect towards closing the deal.

You will notice that the solution is the product - not the price.
Price tags might grab attention, but they don't build lasting relationships.

In a winning sales pitch, the true solution lies beyond a sticker. It's about unveiling how your product transforms lives, tackles challenges, and unlocks potential.

By weaving a narrative of value, you ignite genuine desire, making customers yearn for what your offering can do, not just its cost.

When they finally ask, "how much?" it's not a price inquiry, but a plea to unlock the benefits they can no longer live without.

That's when you know you've crafted a pitch that truly sells. That's what will set you apart from other salespeople - That's what will enable you to smash those targets and prove your worth as a top notch sales person.

That's when you get to Close the sale! But more of that in the next chapter

CHAPTER 6

Step 5 Objections

Objections:
the proverbial elephants in the M7 room. They stalk through every stage, from first contact to closing the deal. But are they roadblocks or stepping stones?

This chapter unravels the dance of objection, revealing how anticipation, empathy, and flexible responses can transform resistance into progress. Buckle up, because addressing an "Can I just stop you there..." as this book is called May just be the detour that leads to your destination, your sale.

But if objections do occur at every stage of the M7 we have already explored, why have I left it til now to discuss? Why do I say this is when they truly arise?

How many times has it happened to you during your initial introduction / customer contact that your prospect has replied, "Can I just stop you there?" Or during your fact find?

They happen, right?

So why am I telling you they happen here at step 5?

I'm telling you that any objections that have arisen before this point are what we know as false objections. Ask yourself, how can they object to anything before you have provided a solution? What exactly are they objecting to?

It is true that objections raised before a solution is presented can often be considered "false objections" in the sense that they don't truly address the merits of the proposed solution itself. Instead, they might be based on pre-existing concerns, misunderstandings, or simply a reluctance to change.

Here are some possibilities for why "objections" might arise before a solution is presented:

> **Lack of information:** Without a clear understanding of the proposed solution, people might feel hesitant or unsure and use general objections as a placeholder for their underlying concerns.
>
> **Misconceptions:** There might be inaccurate information or assumptions about the solution circulating, leading to objections that wouldn't hold up if the solution were properly explained.
>
> **Fear of change:** Some people might be resistant to any new idea, even if it potentially offers benefits, simply because it disrupts the status quo.
>
> **Power dynamics:** Objections could be a way for people to assert their position or maintain control within a group, regardless of the actual merits of the solution.

In all of these cases, it's important to approach the "objections" not as roadblocks, but as opportunities for dialogue and clarification. By actively listening to the concerns being raised, providing more information about the proposed solution, and addressing any misconceptions, it's possible to turn these so-called "false objections" into productive conversations that lead to a better understanding and, potentially, acceptance of the solution.

Remember, the key is to focus on finding common ground and working together to find a solution that everyone can be on board with.

If however, the objections occur here, at stage 5 - after an extensive fact find, after unearthing and establishing a need, after providing a solution- then we can consider these to be 'True Objections', so let's compare True and False objections:

True objections:
- **Emergent:** They arise after building trust and identifying potential fit.
- **Specific:** They pinpoint the exact hurdle preventing forward movement.
- **Motivational:** They signal genuine interest with a need for clarification or reassurance.

False objections:
- **Early blockers:** They surface at the outset, often as brush-offs or excuses.
- **Vague excuses:** They lack specifics and often hide a lack of interest.
- **Time-buying tactics:** They aim to stall discussion, not clarify concerns.

Spotting the difference is crucial. Treat true objections like diamonds: understand their core, tailor your value proposition, and build a bridge to overcome them. Treat false objections like pebbles: acknowledge them calmly, redirect the conversation, and focus on building genuine engagement.

Remember, unlocking true objections fosters trust, strengthens offers, and leads to happier customers.

70% of Salespeople give up after the first objection, but 80% of prospects don't say yes until after the fourth. Read that again!

You're absolutely right! Those statistics are eye-opening. It's true that many salespeople get discouraged by early objections, but understanding what a true objection is and the buyer's journey can make a huge difference.

Here's what we can take from those statistics -

Reframing True objections: It's not a "No," it's an opportunity to address concerns and potentially move forward. This shift in perspective helps salespeople stay motivated and focused on solving the buyer's problem.

Objections at later stages: If an objection comes up after a good conversation and needs assessment, it's a strong signal of interest! The buyer has invested time and effort, indicating their desire to find a solution.

Building the picture: By asking questions and actively listening, salespeople can paint a clear picture of the buyer's needs and demonstrate how their product or service can address them. This builds trust and sets the stage for overcoming objections.

So a good salesperson sees a true objection as a buying sign!

So- knowing that we are faced with actual true objections - how do we handle them, how do we overcome and move forward on our M7?

The AAAA system is a powerful and versatile method for handling objections in sales, negotiations, or any situation where someone expresses opposition.

Let's break down each step:

1. Acknowledge:
This is the cornerstone of effective objection handling. Actively listen to the objection, show empathy, and let the person know you've heard and understood their concern. Use phrases like "Thank you for sharing that," "I understand your hesitation," or "That's a valid point."

2. Ask:
Once you've acknowledged the objection, delve deeper to uncover the underlying reason behind it. This isn't the time to jump in with a defence; instead, ask open-ended questions to clarify their concern. You might say, "Can you tell me more about what worries you about that?" or "What would make you feel more comfortable?"

3. Answer:
This is where you address the specific issue raised in the objection. Use clear, concise language and provide relevant information to address their concern. If necessary, offer options or solutions that demonstrate your understanding and willingness to accommodate their needs. Be sure to tailor your answer to the specific objection and individual you're dealing with.

4. Advance:
Finally, once you've answered the objection, move the conversation forward. This could involve summarising the agreement, asking for their continued interest, or setting a next step. Don't forget to leave them feeling respected and valued.

Remember, the AAAA system is a flexible framework, not a rigid formula. The key is to adapt it to the specific situation and use it in a way that feels natural and authentic to you.

Here are some additional tips for using the AAAA system effectively:

Stay calm and positive: Your attitude can significantly impact the outcome of the interaction.

Maintain eye contact and open body language: This shows you're engaged and interested in what they have to say.

Focus on problem-solving: Be a collaborative partner, not an adversary.
   Don't interrupt or belittle their concerns: Listen attentively and show respect.

Be mindful of your tone of voice: Speak clearly and avoid sounding condescending or defensive.

By following these tips and mastering the AAAA system, you can confidently and effectively handle objections, ultimately leading to more successful interactions and outcomes.

So, we've grasped recognising true objections.
We're ready to move onto the next step of the M7..

CHAPTER 7

Step 6 Close

Having effectively navigated and mastered the M7 sales track, established a need, addressed and overcome objections, the ultimate goal is to move the prospect towards a decision. And hearing them ask about cost is a clear indicator of their purchase interest.

Now, choosing the right closing technique depends on your specific situation and the prospect's signals. Here are a few options to consider:

1. Assumptive Close:
Confidently assume the sale is moving forward and ask about next steps, like "Great! When would you like to get started with implementation?"

2. Alternative Close:
Offer two choices, both leading to a purchase, like "Would you prefer the standard package or the one with the extended warranty?"

3. Trial Close:
Test the waters with a smaller commitment, like "Would you be interested in a free trial to see how it fits your needs?"

4. Urgency Close:
Highlight a limited time offer or potential loss to create a sense of immediacy, like "This special discount expires tomorrow, so let's lock it in now."

5. Summary Close:
Briefly recap the key benefits and value you've discussed, then ask, "Does this seem like a good solution for your needs?"

Remember, the best closing technique is a natural continuation of your conversation, not a forced pitch. Focus on building value and addressing any remaining concerns the prospect might have.

It's also important to be prepared to discuss pricing openly and transparently. Have your pricing information readily available and be ready to explain the value proposition behind your different options.

Ultimately, the goal is to guide the prospect towards a confident purchase decision that leaves them feeling satisfied and excited about the outcome. And moves you to smashing your goals!

Close the deal with confidence! Remember, by completing the M7 steps you have successfully established the need, you have provided the tailored made solution, and you have addressed and overcome any objections that have been thrown at you.

When the price question pops up, that's your cue to shine.
Exude positivity, highlight your solution's value, and offer options.

You've earned the right to ask for the sale, and with the right approach, it's yours for the taking. Don't be afraid to close the deal - you've got this!

CHAPTER 8

M7: Follow Up - Building Lasting Relationships

Congratulations! You've closed the deal and secured a new client. But remember, in the world of sales, the real win lies in building long-term relationships.

Here's why the follow-up is crucial:

From Transaction to Trust:
A one-time sale is good, but a loyal customer is gold. By following up, you transform a quick transaction into a trusting partnership. This client will not only remember you for future needs, but might also become a source of valuable referrals, bringing in new business through positive word-of-mouth.

Unveiling Hidden Gems:
This client might have additional needs beyond the initial purchase, or they could be connected to someone who does. By maintaining contact, you uncover these hidden opportunities before your competitors even have a chance.

Loyalty is King:
People prefer to do business with those they know and trust. Following up demonstrates that you care about their success story, not just the sale. This fosters loyalty, leading to repeat business and a steady stream of revenue.

Taking Action:
1. Schedule it in:
Block a call in your calendar to follow up with this client every 3 months. Consistency is key.

2. Personalise the Contact:
Don't send generic emails. Craft a personalized message that shows you remember their specific needs and goals.

3. Offer Value:
Focus on providing value beyond just selling. Share relevant articles, industry updates, or success stories that could benefit their business.

4. Be a Resource:
Position yourself as a trusted advisor, readily available to answer questions and offer support.

Remember: By following up and nurturing the relationship, you become a valuable partner in their journey.

This builds trust, fosters loyalty, and increases the chances of them turning to you for future needs, choosing you over a stranger every single time.

So go forth, connect, and build a network of loyal clients – that's the true mark of a sales champion!

SUMMARY

And it's a wrap!

You have now completed the full M7 sales strategy! Here's a breakdown of each step and the general principles of sales:

1. Planning and Prep:
Planning and Prep is absolutely a crucial first step in many strategies, including sales. It aligns perfectly with the concept of M7 being adaptable because strong planning and preparation are fundamental to success across many endeavours.

2. Customer Contact:
This involves establishing initial communication with the potential customer. This could be a cold call, email outreach, or following up on a lead.

3. Fact Finding:
Here, you delve into understanding the customer's situation. This might involve asking questions about their needs, challenges, current solutions, and budget.

4. Solution:
Based on the information gathered, you present your product or service as the solution to the customer's problems. Highlight how it addresses their specific needs and pain points.

5. Obstacles:
Anticipate and address any objections or concerns the customer might have. Use your product knowledge and preparation from step 1 to overcome these hurdles.

6. Close:
Guide the customer towards making a purchase decision. This could involve offering incentives, outlining next steps, or asking for a clear commitment.

7. Follow Up:
Don't abandon the customer after the initial interaction. Follow up to ensure satisfaction, answer any lingering questions, and potentially explore opportunities for further sales.

This structure aligns well with the strengths of M7:

Adaptability: Each step can be customized based on the specific product and customer.

Clarity: The well-defined steps provide a clear roadmap for the sales process.

Proven Track Record: Each step reflects established sales practices known for effectiveness.

By following the M7 strategy and continuously honing your skills through practice, you'll be well on your way to sales success!

Enjoy your Sales Career!

ABOUT THE AUTHOR

Maz Mitchell, armed with unwavering spirit, plunged into the world of telesales in 1978. The Liverpool Echo's bustling classified department became her training ground, where she honed her skills on unsuspecting ad buyer.

The call centre's vibrant hum called her siren song, and she transformed into a sales trainer, having trained Sales teams not only on UK home turf but also working in Chennai, India training call centres there.
Maz also trained as an actress and appeared in many local soaps, TV dramas and even a few low budget films.

Today, happily retired nestled in the idyllic countryside of Cheshire with her partner and her fur babies, Maz has swapped spreadsheets for sun-dappled trips around Europe in their camper van, and phone pitches for prose. This book, a treasure trove of her hard-won sales secrets, is just the first chapter in her post-retirement adventure.

So, whether you're a sales rookie facing your first dial tone or a seasoned pro seeking a fresh edge, brace yourself for a new journey, climbing the summit of the M7.

Prepare to turn every "no" into a resounding "hell yes!"!
This book, Can I just stop you there – is the first in a series of Sales books form Maz. Look out for her other titles soon!

www.ingramcontent.com/pod-product-compliance
Lightning Source LLC
Chambersburg PA
CBHW071202240526
45470CB00017B/1241

Advanced Wound Care

Techniques and management

By

Chad Peterson

Copyright © 2024

Welcome to "Advanced Wound Care: Techniques and Management," a comprehensive guide designed to elevate the practice of healthcare professionals in the intricate field of wound care. This book is the culmination of my extensive experience and ongoing dedication to advancing patient outcomes through specialized care and evidence-based practices.

This book is tailored for a diverse range of healthcare providers including registered nurses, nurse practitioners, physician assistants, and medical students who are eager to deepen their understanding of wound care. Whether you are just beginning your journey in healthcare or are looking to refine your expertise, this book provides valuable insights and practical techniques that can be applied in everyday clinical settings.

Within these pages, you will find detailed discussions on the latest advancements in wound healing, case studies that highlight critical thinking in complex situations, and step-by-step guides on the most effective treatments. Each chapter is meticulously crafted to ensure you gain not only theoretical knowledge but also practical skills that you can implement immediately.

As practitioners, our primary goal is to enhance patient care. Advanced wound management is a dynamic field requiring a solid foundation of knowledge and a keen ability to adapt to new discoveries and technologies. This book aims to equip you with the tools needed to assess, plan, and manage wound care with confidence and competence.